This book belongs to:

____

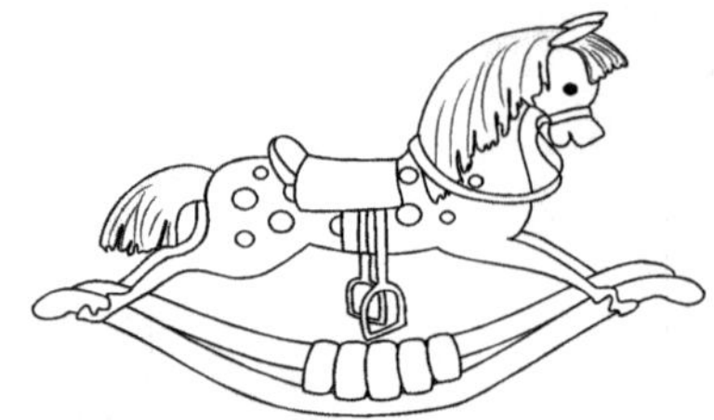

To A Very Sweet Cousin!
Merry Christmas
Coloring Card

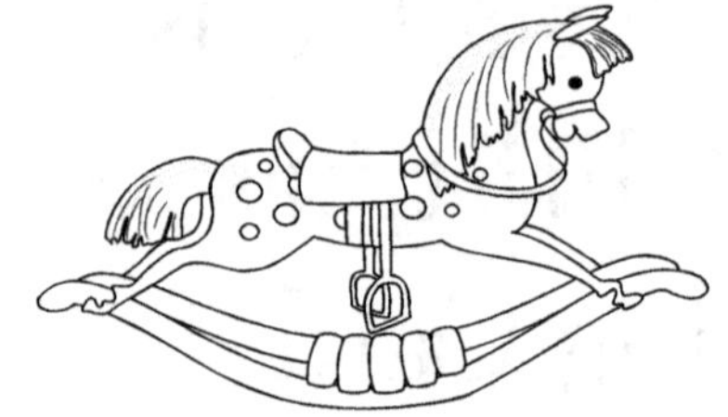

Joy to the world!

Warm wishes to you!

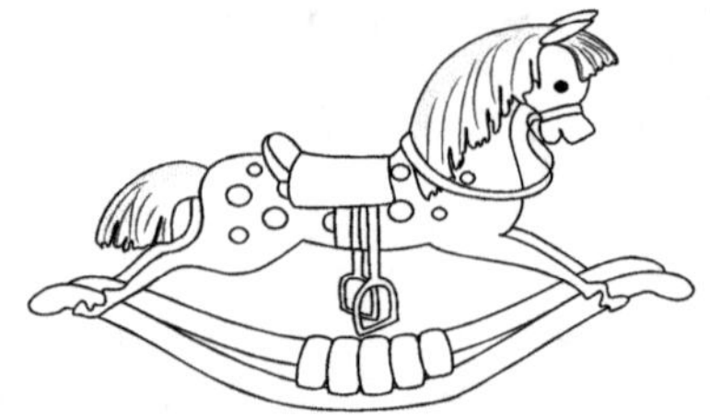

Merry and Bright!

Tis the season to be jolly,
fa la la la la la la la lamb!

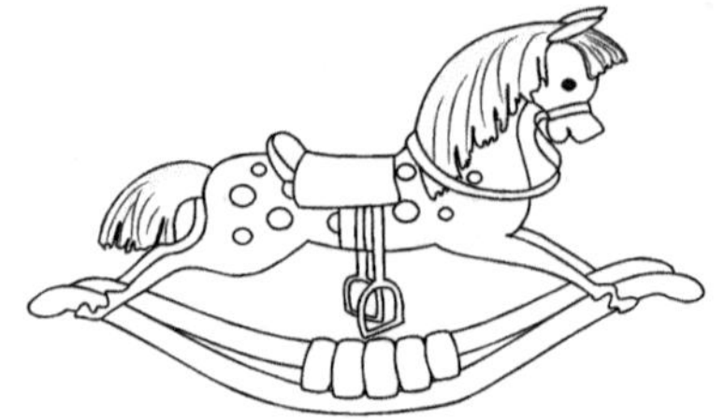

It's the best Christmas ever!

Joy to the animals!

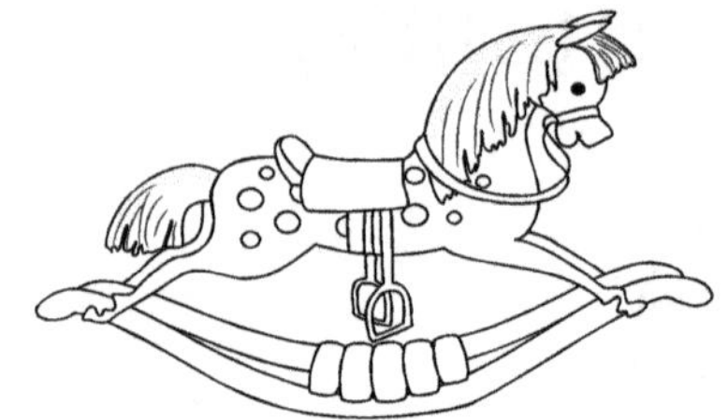

Santa's magic reindeer!

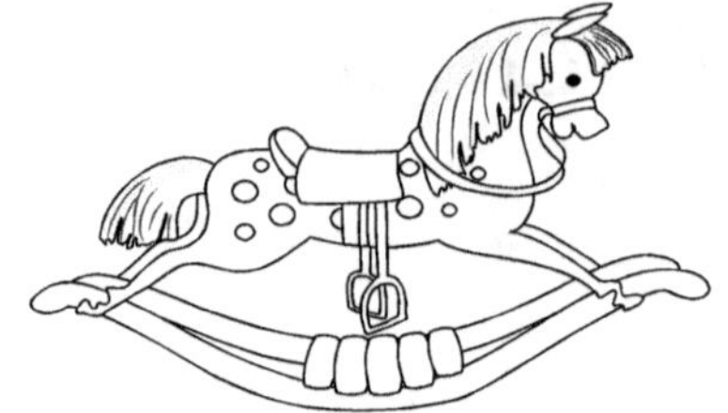

One of Santa's helpers!

Flying in a winter wonderland!

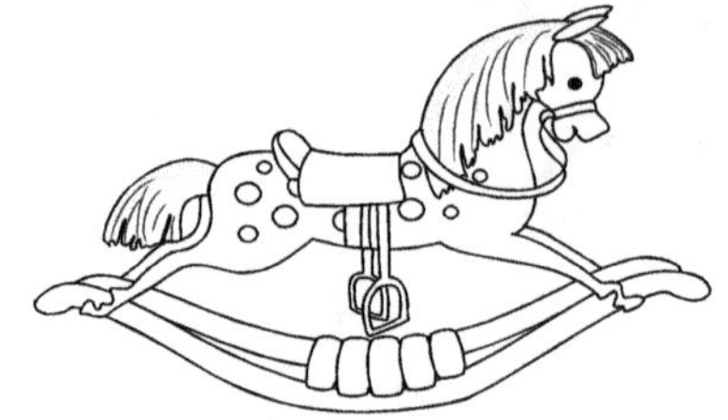

To A Very Sweet Cousin!
Merry Christmas
By Florabella Publishing, LLC